Piano
Grade 2

Pieces & Exercises
for Trinity College London exams

2015-2017

Published by
Trinity College London
www.trinitycollege.com

Registered in the UK
Company no. 02683033
Charity no. 1014792

Gavotte

William Boyce
(1711-1779)

Ländler

Franz Schubert
(1797-1828)

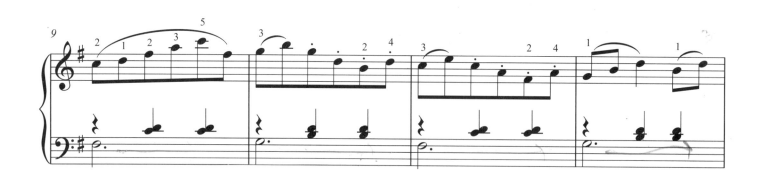

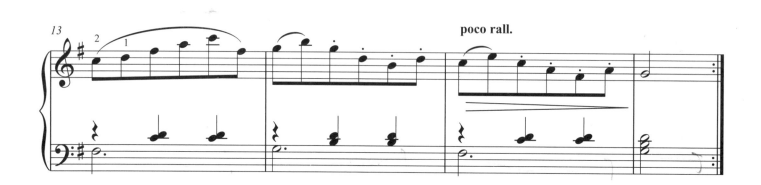

4

Allegro un peu louré

from *Giselle*

Arr. Janet and Alan Bullard

Adolphe Adam
(1803-1856)

Willow, tit-willow

from *The Mikado*

Arr. Janet and Alan Bullard

Arthur Sullivan
(1842–1900)

Mexican March

David Cullen
(born 1942)

Street Beat

Alan Bullard
(born 1947)

FreuDich / Feelicitous

Michael Proksch
(born 1958)

All dynamics are editorial

The Penguin Parade

Christine Donkin
(born 1967)

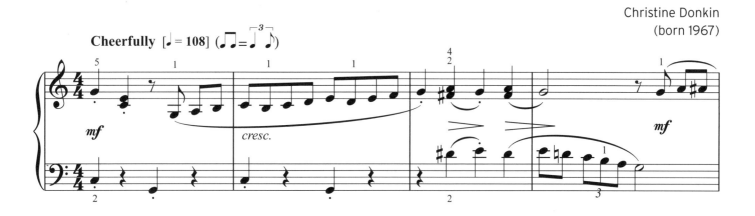

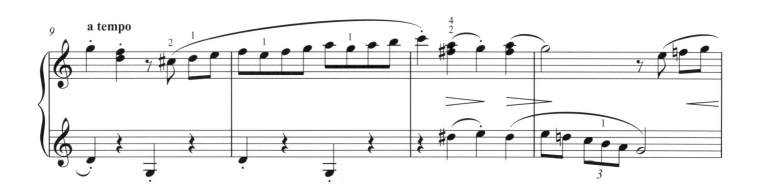

Composer's original metronome mark is ♩ = 126

The Swing Detectives

Ben Crosland
(born 1968)

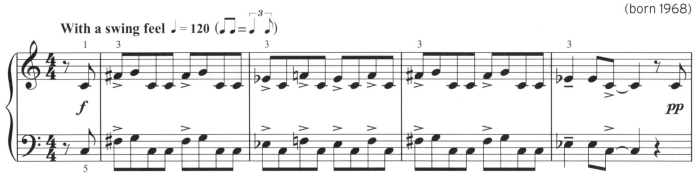

12

Exercises

1a. Revolving Door – tone, balance and voicing

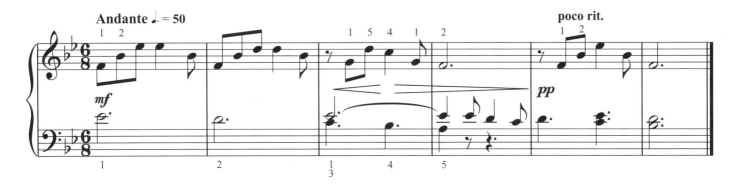

1b. No Reply – tone, balance and voicing

2a. Hot Coals – co-ordination

2b. Pins and Needles – co-ordination

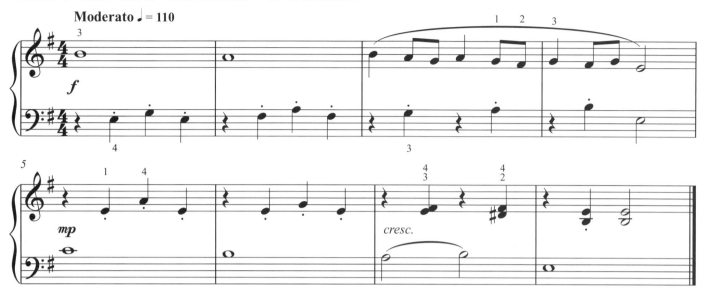

3a. Chill Factor – finger & wrist strength and flexibility

3b. Creepy Goings-on – finger & wrist strength and flexibility

14

Teaching notes

Boyce　　　　Gavotte　　　　　　　　　　　　**page 3**

The page looks quite busy, but worry not! This gavotte is in ternary form, with an exact repeat of the opening eight bars at the end. What's more, there are several patterns that are repeated, like the descending thirds in bars 5–7, and the broken chords in bars 10–11. William Boyce was a highly respected English composer of the 18th century and he knew what he was doing!

Much of the musical detail is editorial, but the *grazioso* direction reminds us that this is a dance, beginning, as all good gavottes should, on the third beat of the bar. The pattern is generally one of two upbeats leading to a slightly stressed first beat of a bar, initially emphasised by a slur in the bass. Then the second phrase looks further ahead, running in one long line from the upbeats to bar 5 until it temporarily rests in bar 8. It would be logical to feel a *crescendo* through these bars, so start a little under **mf** to enable this. The middle section is admittedly a little more crowded, with the harmony changing more frequently, necessitating precise, clear fingerwork in both hands. Although much articulation has been suggested, there are still decisions to be made: eg the quavers in bars 12–15 (*legato* is most straightforward) and the bass crotchets in bars 5–7 (perhaps slightly detached but not *staccato*). Finally, the overall impression needs to be one of ease. A display of effort in a courtly dance would have been frowned upon, so aim for the same effect in the music.

Schubert　　　　Ländler　　　　　　　　　　**page 4**

This Ländler makes use of a mere two chords, tonic and dominant, yet the music is alive with interest and variety. This comes from his avoidance of a downbeat chord in the first section, meaning that the second and third beat chords should be light and unaccented, whereas in the second section we get a *forte* sustained bass note, suddenly adding depth and sonority to the texture. Ländlers often featured stamping, or slapping of the thighs, and perhaps this is what is being suggested here. The melodic line is busy, outlining broken chords, covering quite a range, and barely stopping for breath. Excellent fingerwork practice for the right hand. This is most definitely instrumental music, not Schubert's home territory of the Lied, and the regular phrasing in the first section resembles the fresh bow or the tonguing of a violin or clarinet. With the bass sustaining in the second part, the melody is free to jump around more, which it does. Remember that the second note in a slur will be lightly released, but not have the same edge as a bona fide *staccato*. No repeats in the exam, just a gentle *rit. e dim.* to bring this dance to a close.

Adam　　　　Allegro un peu louré　　　　**page 5**

This is the music for Giselle's first entrance. *Giselle* may be a typically romantic ballet, but the music for this dance needs to have a steady pulse. The mood is light-hearted and the dancer has quite a lot of jumping to negotiate. No repeats in the exam, but a definite *più mosso* starting on the last quaver of bar 18.

To help the feeling of lightness, keep the left-hand quavers very much in the background in the first two sections. The right hand should use a drop-float action on the slurred quaver pairs, with the second note of the slur being lighter and having less bite than the following two *staccato* quavers. The dynamic scheme reflects a sense of growing confidence: Giselle begins a little tentatively, but is more sure of herself by bar 11, and positively beams with happiness as the music gets faster and she shows off more complicated steps. The articulation is almost always the same in both hands, so the bass should also play *staccato* for the last two quavers of bar 25, but the next quavers, in **ff**,

can be a little longer. Be sure to use the arms for those last three chords. A good arrangement of this dance, fitting very well under the hands yet sounding satisfyingly full.

Sullivan　　　　Willow, tit-willow　　　　　**page 6**

An excellent sense of pacing is needed for this aria from Gilbert and Sullivan's *The Mikado*. Ko-Ko is trying to persuade Katisha to marry him, and he wins her heart by telling her the story of a bird who died for love. The song is poised, wistful and delicate. The words can easily be found on the internet, and we should recognise the part W S Gilbert played in writing the immortal words: 'tit-willow', that are set so tenderly here, always remembering that this is a comedy!

Two thumbs, staying close on the keys and playing on the flesh of the finger, will probably play those opening repeated Ds most gently. Note that some semiquaver upbeats, for instance to bar 3, are articulated, whereas some, such as those in bar 8, are slurred. The left hand also has detail to be aware of: the sustained bass and shapely tenor line in bars 1–2; the tie in bar 9 versus the slur in bar 10; and the quaver in bar 16, which will release while the melody sustains until the middle of the bar. The *una corda* at the end would be useful to help achieve the **pp**, but not essential if the pianist cannot reach it, or you are using a keyboard without one; just control the tone with your fingers. The music becomes more impassioned from bar 8 to the climax in bar 14 – a small easing of the tempo into this is usual when it is sung. But then a return to the sorrowful bird call 'tit-willow, tit-willow, tit-willow', which is most effective if played absolutely in time.

Cullen　　　　Mexican March　　　　　　　**page 7**

The speed is only moderate, but this is full of energy, needing firm, decisive playing. Keep the dotted rhythms tightly precise: unlike the easy-going swung quavers for our detectives in *The Swing Detectives*, these Mexicans are disciplined and march in close formation!

There is a different *staccato* for most occasions and often we tend to play *staccato* notes too short. But here I feel a crisp, pointed *staccato* is just what is needed. In contrast, the thirds towards the end could be *non legato*, and all the crotchets should be held for almost their full length. To achieve the *fortissimo* on the top A in the last bar, you may want to play it with the right-hand thumb, or perhaps even with the left hand; it needs to sound like the climax of the whole piece. The repetitions in this will make it a relatively easy choice, but although there are lots of loud accents, listen to ensure that the sound is never ugly.

Bullard　　　　Street Beat　　　　　　　　　**page 8**

I can imagine this will be a popular choice. It is both fun to play and is not too demanding. In ternary form, ABA, there's a great sense of the whole street band joining in when the right hand moves up an octave for the return of the opening tune. A real contrast between the A and B sections should be clearly audible: **mf** and **f** in A, largely **p** in B; smooth playing of the melodic fragments in A, but a light detaching of the notes in B. Along with the louder tone, there are also accents marked in A – no elegant phrasing off here – whereas in B the last notes of each four-note group are crotchets, so will be longer but un-accented. Those bass chords will not take long to learn, but listen for perfect synchronisation of the three notes, keeping the hand close to the keys, and, as always, check that they are not obscuring the right hand melody (except for bar 7). A surprise ending adds the final touch to make this a sure winner in performance.

| Proksch | FreuDich/Feelicitous | page 10 |

A strange title indeed! 'Freu dich' means 'be happy' or 'rejoice' and this is definitely a piece that lifts the spirits. In the bright trumpet key of D major the left hand bounces away on quavers, while the right hand weaves a seemingly never-ending line that refuses to leave the tonic key for a single moment. Its energy and interest comes from the ever-changing articulation patterns, sometimes beginning a bar with a *staccato*, and sometimes playing smoothly over the bar line. It is worth spending a little time spotting the differences between the two halves. Editorial dynamics have been added, the point being to encourage performers to make each half sound different. You can also play around with the fingering: I like using the same fingering on similar patterns, so would play all three groups of semiquavers in the first two bars with 1, 2, 3, despite the F sharp. At this tempo the *forte* largely needs to be created by energised, strong fingers, working from a good bridge. It's perhaps a shame that the roles of the hands are not reversed midway, but this is indeed a joyous piece that will also give the right hand an excellent workout.

| Donkin | The Penguin Parade | page 11 |

Another piece that lives on the lighter side of life. Completely delightful and gently cheeky. Swung quavers, as befits a penguin waddle: meaning that we play them as the first and third of three triplet quavers rather than as equal pairs. It is in binary form, but Donkin has made some clever alterations in the second part. Whereas the first two bars are based around a tonic chord of C, when the opening returns things are changed so that these bars sit on the dominant, a chord of G. Similarly the second four-bar phrase in section A uses sequence to build suspense, ending with a *forte* question mark in bar 8. After a pause and a short break (note the comma), we begin again, but now the second phrase of section B is one long *crescendo*. This sounds to me like a long slide down a chute into the water, perhaps by an inexperienced penguin, who belly flops with the accents. A lot of phrases in the right hand begin on upbeat quavers with a thumb, so keep your ears open to check that these thumbs begin without accents, leading into the next downbeat. And don't tell anyone I suggested it, but you could try playing the three groups of quavers from bar 14-15 all with the right hand, lifting at the end of each group. The end justifies the means, so see which fingering works better for you.

| Crosland | The Swing Detectives | page 12 |

Along with the Alan Bullard, this will be another popular choice, tapping into a bluesy harmonic language and using a relaxed 'swung', triplety rhythm. Just as with the Bullard, there is a surprise ending. Perhaps try starting the *p* subito with thumbs in both hands, helping the accent, as well as using a comfortable mirror fingering. If you then play the fourth bass note with a thumb, you will easily reach the low C, using the full weight of your hand/arm to make the sudden *sfz*.

The whole piece is played *non legato*. Quite a heavy, swaggering, hip-swinging, nonchalant articulation at the opening, with accents exactly as marked. The sudden *pp* will take some controlling: let the arms feel much lighter here, especially in the bass, and the accents must disappear. Bar 8 is a bit of a conundrum, with the *tenuto* marks making the *diminuendo* from *pp* rather a challenge. If you think of the *tenutos* as telling you that these descending notes momentarily take over the audience's attention, they make more sense. That *p* at the very end of bar 12 is crucial, enabling you to grow through the last line. I'm not sure how efficient these detectives would be at detecting – they seem to be having far too much of a good time!

| Arnold | Gigue | *Faber* |

This will give the right-hand fingers a good workout. Although the left hand has fewer quavers, it still plays an important supporting role – and they too win prizes at the Oscars! A simple sequential pattern takes the hand down an octave, with the third finger crossing over the thumb. Make this as smooth as possible, phrasing off at the end of the fourth bar and moving the arm quickly to take the hand back up to the original position. If you grab at this with the fingers, you will get an unnecessary accent; the arm does the heavy lifting, leaving the fingers free to play the quavers.

The arpeggio in the bass at the end of each section would have an extra injection of energy if these quavers were articulated, slightly detached, although with a long dotted crotchet. The left-hand quavers in bar 12 could work either with a *diminuendo* and a *subito f* in the next bar, or you could *crescendo* through them into the last phrase. Remember that it is the speed at which the note is depressed that determines the dynamic, so the fingers want to feel lively and powerful for the *forte*, then lighter and lazier for the *piano* (without changing tempo of course). Listen for the rests in the left hand – their precision also gives energy – and feel the sense of dance that underpins the piece. A small misprint: the first note in the bass should be a dotted crotchet. A tempo of around 100 dotted crotchets a minute will fulfil the *allegro con brio* direction.

| Attwood | Andante | *OUP* |

Thomas Attwood has a distinguished pedigree. A chorister at the Chapel Royal, a pupil of Mozart's in Vienna, organist at St Paul's Cathedral, and one of the first professors of the Royal Academy of Music. It is for his church music that he is now most well known, and this piece could well have been an early composition exercise for his teacher Wolfgang Amadeus if it didn't have such a late date.

With an Alberti bass at a relatively high pitch, some pedal would warm the sound. It is not essential, but any pianist who is already comfortable with *legato* pedalling could try changing every crotchet here. With twice as many notes in the bass to the right hand it will be important to modify the *piano* dynamic, making the melody *mp* or the accompaniment *pp* so that the tune is clearly projected. I like to separate the I-V-I bass at the cadences, pointing the cadence, but whether you play them smooth or detached, there must be a *diminuendo* through these bars. There is no change of dynamic marked for the middle section, but the relative major key of F would be well-served by a slightly brighter tone, allowing an effective softening as you approach the return of the opening theme. Gentle, but rather touching; perhaps more the work of a master than an apprentice after all. Try it at around ♩ = 92.

| Bullard | Flying Above the Clouds | *OUP* |

This is immensely atmospheric, like the dream of a waltz where your feet never quite touch the ground. But, ironically, it should only be played if the pianist can comfortably reach the pedals, keeping the heel on the ground. Bullard is astutely asking for direct pedalling, as a step on the way to later *legato* pedalling, meaning that the pedal is depressed with the first crotchets of every two bars, then released with the fifth. The exception is at the end, where the pedal is held until the last note dies away.

As the melody floats above the hazy chords at the top of the stave, so the arm also feels it is gliding, following the shape of the line through a supple wrist. Bullard has notated some phrasing and dynamic shaping, but the whole piece sounds as though it is in two long breaths, like birds floating on the thermals, following the invisible shape of the breeze. Practise the left hand as chords and try singing the melody on top. One in a bar, with no feeling of verticality or of rigour in the pulse. Just under a ♩. = 60 will be a good tempo.

Hässler   Allegro   *OUP*

This is a piece that lifts the spirits, with its bright C major, its buoyant articulation and the rippling semiquavers that so cleverly fit under the hand. It should be lively rather than fast; ♩ = 88 or thereabouts. There are no definitive ways of approaching the articulation, but probably most quavers should be detached unless actually marked with a slur, with a more pointed *staccato* where directed. The opening fanfare sounds strong if the quavers are quite long, whereas those in the bass in bars 11 and 12 sound good if light and short. Hold crotchets for their full length and play all semiquavers with a bubbly *legato*.

Although the opening is marked *f*, there seems to be a natural sense of growth through bars 1–5. Similarly it would make sense to play bars 11–12 with a different dynamic shading to bars 9–10, perhaps less loud to allow a gradual *crescendo* back to *forte* on the last line. Although this is in a celebratory mood, it is still from the classical period, and there should be an intrinsic elegance in the sound and phrasing. *Forte*, yes, but not heavy. Notice the graceful ending of the first section, the need to phrase away from the bass in the final bar. These are hallmarks of the writing of this period and observing these unwritten rules will show an understanding of this more restrained style.

Seiber   Jazz – Etudiette   *Faber*

A piece that will appeal to many, but the continuous *staccato* quavers, a little akin to tongue-twisters at times, will not suit everyone. The tempo marked on my edition is 96, which is very sedate, and I would suggest 160 better captures the mood, and satisfies the 'etudiette' part of the title. A finger *staccato* would be most economical, but a small hand *staccato*, given the *p* dynamic, also works well. Keep close to the keys and, as always, imagine an air bubble in the wrist, no stiffness there whatsoever. Allow the dynamic to follow the shape of the music: a little less in the lower bars 3–4, then a build back up to *p* and beyond during bars 5–8. Learn the bass as chords before breaking into separate notes (you will need to play two chords in bars 7 and 15). The syncopated treble should not prove a problem for most young children, who find these jazzy rhythms very easy to assimilate and reproduce.

Seiber is another folksong-collecting Hungarian, who worked in Germany for some while before fleeing the Nazis and settling in England. He taught at Morley College in London and wrote two sets of characterful 'Easy Dances' for piano from which this piece comes.

Spindler   Waltz   *OUP*

This is a gem: elegant, sparkling and perfectly balanced. Not the easiest option at this level, and it is also quite long – be prepared to play the *da capo*, but don't be surprised if the examiner needs to stop after the trio. Because the first section is so long, you do need to play the repeat in the trio for the structure to make sense.

There are features here that you will meet throughout your piano-playing life. For instance the waltz accompaniment: a slight lean is needed on the bass note, then the next two chords should be light and unobtrusive. Classical phrasing: the first two bars lead to the dominant, then the next two relax back onto the tonic. Then comes the four-bar phrase, gently flirting with the minor, but cadencing firmly back in the tonic, C major. A melodic snippet in G is answered at a higher pitch, then, higher still, a sequence takes us to A minor, then down the right hand and falls back to G. And so on... The tonal changes that come as a result of understanding this narrative are too subtle to notate, but are implicit in the music and you will show much sophistication if your interpretation includes them. The trio is in the subdominant, and seems more subdued in mood and colour. Let the length of the chords reflect this, with bars 26 and 28 making a small *diminuendo* as indicated by the slur. A crotchet pulse of around 126 is good, but aim to feel one in a bar.

Tanner   Walrus Rag   *Spartan*

Another of Tanner's gently witty animal pieces, with flattened blue notes and some catch-you-out rhythms. At this level, it would be more practical to slur the triplet into the following crotchet, checking that the thumb, with which you will probably begin the triplet, knows that it must play the lightest note of the four. Tanner has not asked for a swung rhythm, so although you could play the dotted rhythm in bars 10 and 20 a little more lazily than usual, the quavers (ie those that are not triplets) should keep their 'duplet' rhythm intact. Do walruses clap their flippers, or is that just sea lions? Whichever, the accents in bars 8, 18 and 24 could well be wet, explosive claps, although the rather sprightly triplets and *staccato* bass don't really reflect a walrus's normally considerable weight! The rests in bars 5–8 must be meticulously correct; elsewhere thinking in minims is good, but here you should subdivide into crotchets (or even quavers) to hold that pulse steady. Rests like these are not absences; they are full of tension and possibility.

Telemann   Fantasy   *Faber*

Written in the warm colour of B♭ major, this fantasy is in ternary form and has the characteristics of a stately dance. This may still be a relatively rare key at this stage, so spend some time checking the scale, arpeggio and primary triads. In fact this is an ideal piece to become more familiar with the chords, as they are the basis for most of the melodic material, and also the reason for this fantasy being somehow so satisfying. The first and third sections simply use I and V7, while the central section briefly visits E♭ major and F major, before a suggested slight pulling back of the tempo returns us to the opening music. This baroque piece has been heavily edited in this version and pianists can choose to use their own dynamic scheme and phrasing, bearing in mind the tonal narrative.

Telemann was born just a few years before Bach and Handel, both of whom he knew, later becoming godfather to C P E Bach. We can see in this simple two-part writing how more complex baroque counterpoint is giving way to an early classical style. No need for repeats in the exam and a tempo of dotted minim = 60 should help pianists feel the two compound beats per bar.

Williams   Hedwig's Theme   *Faber*

There's a reason why John Williams is one of the most respected film composers, and here it is: exquisite, memorable, inspired writing. The only thing amiss on this page is the comic drawing of Hedwig. The actual music is sophisticated and seems to capture the swooping flight of the owl and its age-old wisdom. If pianists are already able to use the pedal, then a touch here and there will add to the atmosphere of gliding through the night air, but it is not at all necessary.

Above all, this requires a good *legato*. Keep the wrist supple so that the arm can help – there is quite a lot of movement over the keyboard, so you want to check that the arm is always in place behind the fingers, and not locked at the elbow. This is especially necessary in bar 7, where there is a tricky octave leap. If the right hand cannot stretch this, then you could play the lower D♯ with the left, making sure the integrity of the melodic line is not disturbed. Listen to the semiquavers; they must sing as part of the line and not be hurried over, nor accented. A small *rit.* as Hedwig disappears over the horizon in the final bar.

Teaching notes written by Pamela Lidiard

Key

A solid line denotes a piece within this book.

A dotted line denotes a piece from the alternative list.